MARRIAGE ETIQUETTE

MARRIAGE ETIQUETTE

HOW TO ARRANGE
A WEDDING

By

"Best Man"

The Engagement
Wedding Preparations
The Marriage Ceremony
Parents' Responsibilities
Duties of the Bridesmaids and Best Man
The Reception—Toasts and Speeches
Honeymoon Arrangements

INCLUDES THE REVISED PROVISIONS FOR
SCOTTISH & ANGLO-SCOTTISH MARRIAGES

LONDON

W. FOULSHAM & CO., LTD.

NEW YORK   TORONTO   CAPE TOWN   SYDNEY

W. FOULSHAM & CO. LTD.
Yeovil Road, Slough, Bucks, England

ISBN 0-572-00188-6

MADE IN GREAT BRITAIN
BY JOHN GARDNER (PRINTERS) LTD., LIVERPOOL 20
© W. FOULSHAM AND CO. LTD. 1971

MARRIAGE ETIQUETTE

CONTENTS

Contents

MARRIAGE ETIQUETTE

Chapter I

THE ENGAGEMENT

Despite the cynics who liken the married state to a beleaguered city where those outside are trying to get in, and those inside trying to get out, marriage is an institution which it must be admitted has stood the test of time, and will continue to rank with birth and death as one of the most important events in human destiny, until life itself becomes extinct upon our planet.

It is impossible to analyse the mutual attraction which draws any particular couple together, nor is it necessary since God Himself is answerable for it. "Man and Woman created He them", and the bond between them is the Love which was breathed into Adam and Eve, the first lovers in the world. But since it is so often the little things in life which cause happiness or sorrow, there is every need for the lover and his lady to learn, study and practise the details of correct behaviour from the time of the proposal to the day of the wedding, if they would walk a smooth and peaceful path to a golden wedding in every sense of the phrase.

It is hardly necessary to warn young people of the present day against entering lightly into such important matters as love and marriage; modern conditions of life have unfortunately almost succeeded in putting "old heads on young shoulders" in this respect, but it is as well to impress on the mind of all those who are interested in love-making that to allow a passing attraction to express itself, and then "cool off", is a cruel and dangerous proceeding. It is only fair for either man or girl to reserve and conceal any easily aroused affection until a reasonable test of its likely endurance and suitability has been made.

When the modern Adam and Eve are definitely decided on this point, there is but one thing more to be said on the subject, and this is merely a reminder that all courtship should be acknowledged as a preparation for a happy marriage, not, as so many lovers have mistakenly made it, an end in itself. The greatest adepts in love-making frequently prove themselves the greatest failures in marriage, and it is worth a little time and consideration of such an important matter to discover whether the prospective partner is a true lover or only an effective love-maker.

The fiancé who is considerate in little ways, and

candid over financial matters, is more to be trusted than the perfect lover whose gifts are as extravagant as his compliments are profuse.

When, however, an engagement has been entered upon, and some insuperable difficulties encountered either through the discovery of a faulty character on the part of one of the lovers, or force of circumstances, it is kinder to break the engagement definitely and immediately, than to linger in a state either of dissatisfaction or vacillation, for fear of a temporary infliction of pain to the partner in the engagement, or passing annoyances in the way of the world's comments and criticisms.

There are few griefs of this kind which a few months' absence and a few miles' distance will not ease. A clean cut soon heals, while a sore of long standing may prove incurable.

Very young girls frequently hesitate to break an engagement with a man of unsuitable character, on the plea that he may reform when married to a good woman, and will certainly "go to the bad", as he probably threatens to do, if she "throws him over".

This is a false and dangerous argument since the very fact that the lover can use such a plea proves his incurable weakness. A strong character would overcome his faults before permitting the woman he loved to become his wife. It is infinitely kinder as well as more sensible for a girl to discuss with her lover a serious fault—such as the drink habit, or financial difficulties due to past debts—giving him a definite period in which to overcome his unsuitability before a marriage can be considered. On the other hand some admirably suited couples may hesitate to marry on account of some inequality of position. This also is inadvisable, since where the bond of affection is strong, worldly obstacles will be found easier to surmount than serious faults of character.

For two unrelated human beings really to know one another is, however, a difficult matter, and it is only natural that quite unfounded suspicions should sometimes mar a possible romance. Men are often reticent creatures, not given to talking of their past lives, their relations, or even their daily occupations when in the throes of a serious love-affair, and it is as well for a girl to ascertain tactfully whether such reticence arises from a secretive nature, shyness, or some fact of which he is ashamed; in the latter case it being of the utmost importance to clear up the matter before entering upon a definite engagement.

When an attracted pair have arrived at feelings of mutual understanding and affection, there arises for the man in the case the sometimes difficult task of proposing marriage. To a sensitive nature, this often causes the utmost trepidation, and the only advice which can be given to a bashful lover is to tackle the task with the same courage and skill which he would use in any other emergency, and get it done as quickly and thoroughly as he would if it were a business difficulty. He might do well to remember the romantic but tragic failure of Schubert and his beloved Lili, of whose rejection to his proposal he was so afraid that he actually asked the assistance of a friend. This had the not unnatural result of leading Lili to believe that Schubert was not serious in his intentions, while the friend who sang the song, written by the modest musician for the occasion, made so favourable an impression, that he won the young lady's heart for himself instead of for Schubert. Do not wait then, till the opportune moment has passed, or you may learn that your affection was reciprocated when it is too late.

"Be sure of yourself and make sure of the lady", is the motto for the man. As for the girl, lives there a woman who does not know when a man is in love with her; who has not mentally weighed the pros and cons of his proposal and decided upon her answer even while she disclaims "any idea of that sort"? To the lady in the case, therefore, need only be quoted the well-known verse:

> "To thine own self be true;
> And it must follow, as the night the day,
> Thou canst not then be false to any man".

But on the other hand, while it is foolish as well as cruel to keep a man unhappily waiting to know his fate, it is just as foolish to endeavour to prompt him to make a proposal on which he himself has not yet decided. Such a course has a very unsatisfactory result, despite the privileges and temptations of Leap-year. Only tact and intuition can produce the ideal course, and these cannot be taught; the lovers must be left to help each other as sympathetically and unobtrusively as they can.

Proceeding from the romantic to the more worldly side of getting engaged, the next difficulty in the lovers' path is the attitude of their respective parents. Sometimes it happens most fortunately that the families are on friendly terms, and the engagement is expected and approved long before it actually occurs. Happy are the young people under these circumstances, and in this respect modern lovers are more fortunate than their Victorian predecessors, for few modern parents exercise their legal or moral rights in this important matter. Nevertheless, the fact remains that parents have a definite right to intervene should they disapprove of an engagement, at least until the engaged couple have reached the age of eighteen or obtained legal consent of a magistrate.

The formal procedure is little more than a compliment to the parents, but it cannot be omitted without offence against the code of correct behaviour even in these advanced days. The man who wishes to show respect to his future parents-in-law, should, after having obtained a favourable reply from the girl of his choice, write immediately to her father (or failing him, her mother) asking for an interview. Unless the parent has any special reason for disapproving of his suit, this interview is a mere formality, but it is reasonable for the girl's father to discuss the suitor's prospects and future arrangements before requesting his wife's and daughter's presence and congratulating the young couple. If, on the other hand, one or more of the parents involved should prove "difficult", and the young couple decide to keep their engagement secret rather than run the risk of being separated, half the joy of publicly owning each other's affections is swept away from them and a life of constant pretence becomes necessary.

This is a great pity, and parents should ask themselves sternly whether they are acting from a sense of duty to their children, or merely from a selfish desire to keep them at home as long as possible.

Once having become engaged, however, the next step for the man is to present his fiancée with a ring to grace the third finger of her left hand. This is not made an occasion of ceremony, but is privately chosen and presented during the first weeks of the engagement.

It emphatically is not advisable for a man to buy a ring before having been accepted, as it may suggest over-confidence on his part as to the certainty of his acceptance, which is scarcely likely to please the lady, who would naturally prefer to choose the ring in his company, if possible.

It is a favourite compliment on the man's part to suggest a ring set with his fiancée's birthday jewel, a list of which is given below.

JANUARY	Garnets for Constancy.
FEBRUARY	Amethysts for Sincerity.
MARCH	Bloodstones for Courage.
APRIL	Diamonds for Purity.
MAY	Emeralds for Happiness.
JUNE	Agates for Prosperity.
JULY	Rubies for Fidelity.
AUGUST	Sardonyx for Married Joy.
SEPTEMBER	Sapphires for True Love.
OCTOBER	Opals for Hope.
NOVEMBER	Topaz for Friendship.
DECEMBER	Turquoise for Contentment.

If the girl is not already acquainted with her fiancé's parents, an introduction should no longer be delayed after the ring has been presented, and may be made the occasion of a small dinner-party or week-end visit, if the families live at a distance from each other.

There is, unfortunately, another side to the etiquette of courtship, and that is the mode of procedure when an engagement has proved unsatisfactory. The perfect engagement, like the perfect triangle, should have three equal sides; namely, friendship, suitability and attraction. Either of the two first-named "sides" without the third, makes a lukewarm affection; but the third alone makes a volcanic passion that is almost certain to end (often before the wedding) in the tiring of one or other party to it.

If the "rift within the lute" is only a matter of cooling-off on either or both sides, things may mend themselves by being left alone, since poor health, or a period of over-worked nerves may be responsible for trouble which will prove to be merely a passing one. When, however, there is a good reason for it, such as a serious quarrel, or discovery of unsuitability, the break should be made by the girl and not by the man, as there is always a certain stigma cast upon a woman who has been jilted, while a man in the same circumstances is regarded with sympathy, and usually given "the benefit of the doubt". It is thus a final act of chivalry on the part of a man to give a girl whom he no longer wishes to marry, the opportunity of breaking the engagement.

Etiquette decides that all presents and letters should be returned immediately, although legally, only the engagement ring can be demanded.

When, however, the lovers have parted amicably, it is more polite for each party to write suggesting that there is no need to return either presents or letters. Only an ill-bred person would take the course of writing to demand their return.

Chapter II

WEDDING PREPARATIONS

"A MARRIAGE has been arranged." With the publication of these familiar words, in the columns of the daily papers, begins a whirl of planning, preparation and excitement in the home of the prospective bride. The wording of the announcement should be somewhat similar to the following example:

"A marriage has been arranged (and will shortly take place) between Mr. Andrew Bell, son of Lt.-Col. C. H. Bell, of Cloverley Hall, Plymouth, and Alice, daughter of Mr. and Mrs. G. F. Moore, of Beverley Avenue, Halifax."

The words in parenthesis should be included only if the date of the wedding has been arranged.

It should be remembered, however, that the public announcement is not considered adequate information where near relations and intimate friends are concerned. The engaged couple should make a list of relatives and friends to be told, and write personally to each. Long letters are unnecessary, but formal language, or letters written in the third person, should be avoided.

All letters should be posted at the same time so as to avoid one person hearing the news, before receiving her own intimation, from another whose letter was posted earlier. In answering letters of this kind, the girl should not be congratulated on the occasion, as it is always the man who is supposed to receive the congratulations. It is only necessary to express the pleasure which the information has given to the writer, and wish her happiness in the future.

When the engagement is to be of short duration, friends and relatives will send their presents before the date of the wedding has been announced in the press, and these should be acknowledged immediately. In the event of the engagement being broken off, the presents should be returned promptly. In such circumstances, also, the press announcements must be followed by others to the effect:

"The marriage arranged between Mr. Andrew Bell and Miss Alice Moore will not take place."

The actual wedding must be planned in good time, whether it is to take place in a church, chapel or before a registrar. The bridegroom arranges the details when decided upon, including the date of the ceremony, with the clergyman of the church.

The wedding invitations should be sent two or three weeks before the ceremony is to take place, invitation cards being sent by the bride's parents, although the bridegroom assists in compiling the list. Printed invitations in the third person are necessary and should read somewhat in the following manner:

"Mr. and Mrs. Alfred Moore request the pleasure of the company of Mr. and Mrs. Henry James, at the marriage of their daughter Alice to Mr. Andrew Bell, at Saint Luke's Church, Halifax, on Wednesday, May 18th, at 12.30 p.m."

Should the ceremony be followed by breakfast or a reception, the phrase, or its equivalent, should be added, as:

"and afterwards at a reception at 9 Beverley Avenue, Halifax."

These invitations should be answered by the recipients within three days and in the third person, the reply being sent to the bride's parents. Should congratulations be offered, they should be sent separately, written in the first person and addressed to the bride or bridegroom according to whichever is the better known.

The wedding presents which will follow during the next few days should be sent to the bride—except personal ones intended entirely for the bridegroom—and it is the bride's duty to acknowledge the gifts, though this work is sometimes lightened for her by her mother.

Although the bride's family should send out all invitations to a wedding, even to friends of the bridegroom with whom they may not be acquainted, the bridegroom is privileged to supply his fiancée or her family with a list of his friends and relations whom he wishes to be invited to the ceremony.

When a prospective bride has no mother, the invitations are issued in the father's name; or if both parents are deceased, they are sent in the name of a guardian, an elder brother, a sister who is married, or else much older; otherwise some other relative, or an old friend of the family. Should the bride be making a second marriage, the invitations may be issued by the parents or by the bride herself.

The conventional form of invitation is a double sheet of notepaper , folding to form its own envelope and engraved or printed in silver. It is a mistake to address invitations to "Mr. and Mrs. Smith and family". If the "family" referred to should consist of unmarried daughters, grown-up, but living at home, their names should be added to those of the father and mother, in the invitation; but grown-up, unmarried sons should receive a separate invitation.

A formal acceptance of a wedding invitation (which entails the presentation of a wedding gift) should be worded somewhat as follows:

"Mr. and Mrs. James Smith accept with much pleasure Mr. and Mrs. Moore's kind invitation to the marriage of their daughter Alice to Mr. Andrew Bell at St. Luke's Church, Halifax, on May 18th, at 12.30 p.m."

Should the necessity arise for a postponement of the wedding after the invitations have been sent out, such as a severe illness or death in the family of either of the bridal couple, a notice similar to the following should be sent immediately to everyone invited:

"Owing to the illness (or death) of ———, Mr. and Mrs. Moore regret that they are compelled to cancel the invitation for their daughter's wedding on May 18th."

If a wedding is to take place in the country and guests are expected from some distance, it is customary to add to the invitation, a list of convenient trains, with the words, "Cars will meet these trains".

DRESS

The bridesmaids' dresses are chosen by the bride, but she has no responsibility as to paying for them unless she wishes to make them a personal present. It is customary, however, for the bridegroom to present each of the brides-maids with some small token of appreciation of their assistance. This is usually in the form of an ornament to be worn at the ceremony; such as a brooch, flower-pin, belt-clasp or bracelet.

The bride also chooses the music to be played at the ceremony, and it may be noted that there are other pieces of suitable wedding music besides the well-worn Wedding March of Mendelssohn, although it is the favourite with most brides.

The choice of the bridal gown is a matter of suitability as well as of personal taste, for although the conventional dress is supposed to be of pure white silk or satin, it is considered quite correct at a ceremony taking place in either church or registry office, where there are to be few guests beyond the immediate relations of the couple, to wear an afternoon dress or a costume.

When the bride is married in a hat instead of a veil, it is not customary for her or her bridesmaids to carry bouquets.

In former times it was not thought correct for a lady guest to wear black at a wedding, but this idea has died out, although, unless a guest is still in mourning for a personal loss, it seems somewhat out of keeping with the occasion.

The bridegroom should wear formal attire if his bride is in white. He should not wear much jewellery, a plain gold signet ring and modest tie-pin being all that is in good taste. His conventional wear would be a black or dark grey morning coat, similar or light grey waistcoat, striped trousers, silk hat, a black and white tie of quiet pattern, white shirt, stiff collar, and grey suede gloves.

This fashion is, however, permitted the variation of a black lounge coat, black bowler, or even a light grey felt hat.

WEDDING PRESENTS

Although the conventional wedding presents usually begin to arrive as soon as the invitations to the wedding have been issued, there is really no fixed time which limits their presentation, and it frequently happens, especially amongst intimate friends and relatives of the bridal couple, that they are asked to choose a useful gift for the new home instead of some fanciful present which will be, in all probability, duplicated amongst the formal wedding presents. Whenever received, however, they should be acknowledged immediately.

It is customary to send a present on acceptance of a wedding invitation, and indeed usual whether the invitation is accepted or not, since the fact of receiving an invitation pre-supposes a degree of friendship which makes a present necessary even if circumstances prevent the actual attendance of the giver.

The message accompanying the gift may be either a personal letter, a visiting card, or a special one sold for the purpose, the form of the message being in no way limited by etiquette, but only dictated by the degree of intimacy between the giver and the bridal couple. It may vary, therefore, from "Sincere wishes for your health, wealth and happiness in the future" or "Warmest wishes for your future happiness", to a letter of congratulation and affectionate well-wishing which needs to be composed personally. The card should be tied with white ribbon and if the present is small in size, this also should be tied with a white ribbon or silver cord.

Presents are displayed, as a rule, at the reception, with the sender's card attached to each, so that the ornamental cord has a double purpose; but when a present is too large in size to display, or takes the form of a cheque, a card should be substituted on the wedding-present table bearing the description of the gift, such as:

"Mr. and Mrs. Bell to bride, Cheque," or "Mother to bridegroom, Suite of Dining-room Furniture."

Needless to say, where a valuable collection of presents is displayed, it is advisable to employ a private detective, or "plain-clothes" police officer, for whose services application should be made to the district officer in charge of police, who will estimate the cost and ensure the attendance of such persons.

It is advisable for the bride to make a personal list of the presents received, and from whom, as this will be extremely useful to her for reference later. The bride's parents are usually responsible for their safe removal to the bride's new home.

The question of what to give is a difficult one and only to be solved by the degree of friendship or relationship, resources and needs of giver and recipient. Above all it should be remembered that, like other gifts, the thoughtfulness which prompted it is of more value than the intrinsic worth of the present. This, strangely enough, is not always displayed in the choice of presents. How many young brides-to-be have sighed as they carefully wrote the fifth letter of gratitude for the fifth "beautiful cakestand you so kindly sent", while fervently wishing that one of the five cakestand-givers had been original enough to send "that new-type electric iron I wanted so much".

It is as well to remember that a bride who is going to try the town equivalent to "love in a cottage", will probably bless the giver of a small vacuum cleaner, or other labour-saving contrivance, more gratefully than the sender of the handsome cocktail-set, which is never likely to be used. It is, however, entirely a personal problem only to be solved by attempting to imagine oneself in the position of the prospective bride.

Sometimes a kindly relative will send the bride a list of several suggested presents from which to choose. This is an excellent idea, and the writer once pleased a country bride very much by the gift of a silver table-bell in the exact shape of a wedding bell, engraved with the names of the couple and the date of the ceremony.

Etiquette forbids the selection of a present which is not intended for either the joint use, or joint benefit, of the couple, even if one of the pair is quite unacquainted with the sender. For instance, it would be incorrect for a man friend to send a bride an article of jewellery unless he were some close relative of the bride or bridegroom bestowing some treasured family heirloom upon the young wife; nor should a girl send a wedding present of a personal nature, such as a cigarette or card-case, to a young man about to marry, although a cigarette *box* or card *tray* would be quite acceptable, as either would be of joint household use.

Besides the orthodox bridal gifts of linen, silver or glass, too well-known to need enumeration, the following suggestions might prove useful: coloured blankets to harmonise with the scheme of bedroom furnishings, or for the spare room; an eiderdown, also in the correct colours; garden furniture, such as hammock-chairs, garden umbrellas, cushions; woven-cane table and chairs; a set of waste paper baskets and linen basket in good woven cane to match the colour schemes of the rooms; an electric iron or fire of a modern type; a standard or bedside lamp; an up-to-date kitchen cabinet; set of trays; picnic basket with fittings; gardening tools for a couple who are known to be interested in their garden as a hobby.

There is at least a chance of any of these things being the only gift of their kind, while any of them may be costly or inexpensive according to the funds at the disposal of the giver.

CHAPTER III

THE MARRIAGE CEREMONY

AT one time, weddings could not take place after the hour of 3 p.m., but now this has been altered, so that marriages may be celebrated between the hours of 8 a.m. and 6 p.m. This applies to all forms of marriage, except Jewish weddings—see page 44.

It is an excellent plan at a large wedding, to arrange with the church officials to distribute amongst the guests, leaflets printed with the wedding service, extracted from the Prayer Book, and the names of the bridal pair, with date and name of church, as a souvenir of the occasion.

Visitors should arrive about a quarter of an hour before the time of the ceremony, and bridesmaids with the pages a few minutes later. The latter await the bride in a group at the church door. Several men friends should be requested to conduct visitors to their seats, the bride's friends usually being shown to the left-hand seats of the church, and those of the bridegroom to the right-hand seats facing the chancel.

The bride's mother should reach the church first of the bride's party, and with her any guests who are staying in the house, the bridesmaids and pages coming next, and the bride and her father last. Her mother sits in the front pew on the left of the aisle.

The bridegroom accompanied by his best man should reach the church at least fifteen minutes before the appointed time, and remain in the vestry until a few minutes before the bride's arrival, when they should seat themselves in the front pew to the right of the centre aisle until the bride arrives. The bridegroom then takes his place on the right of the chancel steps with the best man at his right hand, a little behind him.

The bride's train is arranged and taken up by the pages waiting for her at the entrance, and she takes the right arm of her father, or whoever gives her away, before moving forward into the church. The bridesmaids fall into rank behind her as she passes, the chief bridesmaid first, if there should be an odd number, and the rest in pairs, if possible arranged according to height, as this makes for a graceful procession. If it is a fully choral service, the bridal procession will advance to the music of a hymn; at elaborate weddings, preceded by the clergy and choir. When she arrives at the chancel steps where the bridegroom awaits her, the bride takes her place on his left, with the chief bridesmaid at her left hand, a little behind her, the bride's father (or whoever is giving away the bride) remaining on the left of the bride. The chief bridesmaid then takes the bridal bouquet (and gloves if worn) and the bride removes her engagement ring from the left hand to her right until after the ceremony. Sometimes the bride carries an ivory-bound prayer book given by the bridegroom for use on the happy occasion.

In these positions the wedding couple and their attendants remain during the service, but after giving away the bride, her father (or whoever is taking his place) may then step back and sit at her mother's side in the front pew.

The bridesmaids, best man and pages remain where they are while the bride and bridegroom move up to the altar. Either the clergyman or the best man may give the wedding ring to the bridegroom at the proper moment to place it on the third finger of his bride's left hand, but it is most usual for the clergyman to do so, after having received it from the best man.

At the conclusion of the ceremony, the bride takes her husband's left arm, the pages take the bride's train as she leaves the chancel, and they follow the clergyman into the vestry to sign the register and receive the marriage certificate, which is the bride's property. The latter should sign her maiden name in the register before two witnesses; usually the best man and the bride's father or parent from either side.

The chief bridesmaid and the best man, as well as the parents of the bridal pair, also follow into the vestry, where the groom claims the privilege of being the first to kiss his wife, after which congratulations and good wishes are showered upon the newly married pair.

The bridegroom then offers his left arm to his bride, the pages again hold her train, and they leave the church, passing down the aisle to the sound of the Wedding March, followed by the bride's father, who gives his arm to the groom's mother, and the groom's father escorting the bride's mother.

The bride should not be congratulated or stopped as she walks down the aisle, and she should take the first car with her husband, the next being reserved for her mother and father, or her mother and her husband's father as prearranged, followed by the two remaining parents, then the bridesmaids and the guests; the best man leaving in the last car, having seen everyone safely away and completed his few remaining tasks.

When (as in Service weddings) there is a guard of honour, this should be stationed between the church door and the bridal car, making a triumphal arch of swords for the couple to pass beneath.

Country weddings are often made picturesque by a band of flower girls who shower petals in the path of the bridal couple, but the old custom of scattering rice and confetti, or throwing an old slipper, as they leave the church, has been discarded lately owing to the disapproval of the church officials.

CEREMONY BEFORE A REGISTRAR

A Registry Office ceremony is much shorter, the legal requirements being merely a declaration by each of the contracting parties as follows:

"I do solemnly declare that I do not know of any impediment why I, Andrew Bell, may not be joined in matrimony to Alice Moore,"

followed by the statement:

"I call upon these persons here present to witness that I, Andrew Bell, do take thee, Alice Moore, to be my lawful wedded wife."

A similar declaration is made by the bride, reversing the order of the names and substituting the word "husband" for the word "wife".

WEDDING EXPENSES

Despite the fact that modern wedding ceremonies tend to become more simple in style and less costly in outlay, there remains a list of unavoidable expenses which it is as well to estimate beforehand, and tradition makes it incumbent on the bride's parents to be responsible for most of these, while the bridegroom is limited chiefly to the church fees and the provision of the ring and licence.

Except in cases where the social importance of the bridal couple make an elaborate public function indispensable, modern brides are more and more inclined towards the simpler ceremony in which they can wear a smart travelling dress, and big wedding breakfasts are declining in popularity.

Most young people prefer to spend the bulk of their resources on furnishing the new home and starting their married life with a reserve fund, for emergencies, in the bank, so that "Father of the bride—cheque", is more often seen amongst the list of presents than any other form of gift.

In the days when the bride laboriously wrought by hand her own trousseau, except the actual wedding gown—"the bottom drawer" as it was called, consisting of at least six of everything—it was considered the duty of the parents to pay for the household linen; but except in the most old-fashioned of country districts, this idea has lapsed, and it is now one of the duties of the bridegroom to purchase the linen for the new home which it is his special privilege to provide. This change limits the expenses of the parents to the actual cost of the wedding celebration, comprising the newspaper announcements, invitations, bridal trousseau and reception, cars to and from the wedding, the choral service and the floral decorations at the church and reception—which, by the way, need not necessarily be white.

Besides providing the new home and all its

contents, it is the bridegroom's privilege to buy
the wedding ring as well as his own present to the
bride, and her bouquet, pay for the licence, all
church fees and floral or wedding gifts for the
bridesmaids and pages, as well as provide cars for
himself and his best man to and from the church
and also for that in which he and his bride drive
off from the reception. He may use his own car or
provide the one in which the newly-married pair
drive from the church to the reception, but this is
a minor detail to be arranged between him and the
bride's father.

Church marriages are only permitted in the
parish of residence of either of the pair (unless
an Archbishop's Licence, cost £25 (or more),
which allows marriage at any time in any church
has been obtained). Banns must be read in both
churches and a certificate of banns from the
other church handed to the incumbent of the
church of marriage. Or, alternatively, a surrogate's
licence. The last reading of the banns must not
be more than three months before the wedding.
Fifteen days of continuous residence in a parish is
regarded as qualifying for this. The residence
must be genuine. It is not enough to have a
room. It is also permitted for a couple to be married
in any church on the electoral roll of which one
of the pair is registered. The banns must be
read there as well as in both the parishes of
residence.

The cost of getting married in a church is as follows:—

(a) By Banns $\qquad$ £ p.

Publication of Banns $\qquad$ 0.75 To the Minster

0.30 To the Clerk

Marriage Fee after Banns
(where organ not used). $\qquad$ 2.00 To the Minster

1.00 To the Clerk

1.00 To the P.C.C.

Certificate of Banns $\qquad$ 0.50 To the Minster

0.20 To the Clerk

Marriage Fee after Banns
(where organ used)* $\qquad$ 4.00 To the Minister

2.00 To the Clerk

2.00 To the P.C.C.

(b) By Licence $\qquad$ £ p.

Ordinary Licence $\qquad$ 4.50

Marriage Fee after
Licence $\qquad$ 2.00 To the Minister

1.00 To the Clerk

1.00 To the P.C.C.

Subsequent certificate
of Marriage $\qquad$ 0.40

This has nothing to do with the wedding, where there is no charge for the Marriage Certificate.

*This is not inclusive of the organist's fee which is arranged between the Minister and the parties concerned.

(Note: Stamp duty on Ordinary Licences has been abolished.)

The cost of getting married at a Registry Office is as follows:—

(a) By Certificate				£ p.
Entering Notice of Marriage	–	–	–	1.00
Certificate for Marriage –	–	–	–	.50
Marriage Attendance Fee –	–	–	–	1.50
				£3.00

NOTE: If the parties live in different districts, notice has to be entered and a certificate issued by each Registrar, thus increasing the total charges by £1.00.

(b) By Licence			£ p.
Entering Notice of Marriage	–	–	1.00
Certificate and Licence for Marriage –	–	5.00
Marriage Attendance Fee –	–	–	1.50
			£7.50

(Note: Stamp Duty on marriage licences has been abolished.)

The cost of a certified copy of the entry of Marriage—the equivalent of the Certificate of Marriage issued after a marriage in Church—is 50p for marriage by certificate or licence.

Chapter IV

SECOND MARRIAGES

WHILE it is true that a widow on re-marrying has no special legal formalities to attend to, beyond the ordinary ceremonial, there are certain details of etiquette which apply especially to second marriages. For one thing, a widow may issue the wedding invitations in her own name and marry from her own home, although this is not generally done. Usually a friend or relative can be found to act as her chaperone, issue invitations, hold the reception and be her *dame d'honneur* at the ceremony, it being considered incorrect to have bridesmaids or pages at a second marriage. Invitations are worded thus:

"Mr. and Mrs. James request the pleasure of Mr. and Mrs. Henry's company at the marriage of Mrs. Albert Johns with Major Leslie Thompson at Saint George's Church, Bayswater, W., on June 15th, at 12.30 p.m., and afterwards at 18 Queen's Terrace, Notting Hill, W."

It is not customary for a widow to wear white

35

or a bridal veil at the ceremony, as these are the prerogative of maidenhood. Dove grey, mauve or lilac is usually chosen, and her friend, who is *dame d'honneur*, really acts as a bridesmaid. Her first marriage ring must be removed before proceeding to the church or registrar's office. It should not be worn again, out of courtesy to the second husband. There is no rule of etiquette against the bridal cake for a second wedding, nor is there any reason for omitting to invite relations of the first husband to the ceremony or reception if on friendly terms.

This applies also to a woman who has divorced her first husband.

MARRIAGE BY BANNS

The conventional wedding, as described in Chapter III, is usually the method preferred, and is officially known as "marriage by banns". If this form be decided upon, the vicar, or rector, of the church chosen for the wedding ceremony should be called upon and his permission obtained, whether he is desired to officiate or not.

At the same time, if one of the parties should reside in a district other than that in which the marriage is to take place, the clergyman of the church of that parish must also be approached and requested to publish the banns simultaneously. This is a very important point which must not be overlooked.

The preliminaries having been arranged, the clergyman should ascertain that the contracting parties are of age, or have the consent of their parents before proceeding to publish the banns, which is done immediately after the second lesson in the service, on three successive Sundays preceding the ceremony, and should one of the parties live in another parish, it is necessary to obtain a certificate from the clergyman whose church is not to be used, to give to the other clergyman in whose church the ceremony is to be performed, stating that the banns have been called legally. Without this certificate the other clergyman may not proceed with the wedding service.

Should neither of the couple live in the parish in which they wish the wedding to take place, it is usual for the bridegroom-to-be to take a room in that parish and live there during the week-ends, in order to fulfil the requirements of "fifteen days' residence" in the parish, as stated in the certificate. It is not necessary for him to live there every day, but he must sleep there at least one night in each week.

After the banns have been called legally, the wedding may take place on any date within the next three months; but should the ceremony not be performed by the end of that time, the validity of the banns lapses.

The essential reason for the publication of the banns being the prevention of fraudulent marriages, it is important to give the correct name, or the legality of the marriage may be affected. If only one of the parties gives a false name, the marriage is not illegal, but there is danger of imprisonment for perjury to the miscreant, as it constitutes fraud against the Crown. Therefore anyone who is more generally known by a name not his or hers legally should include both on the banns, as for instance, "Ethel (Queenie) Smith".

When, as sometimes happens, one of the parties frequents a certain church not in the parish in which either lives, and wishes to be married there, the banns may be published and the wedding performed there (provided by an Act of Parliament, 1930).

MARRIAGE BY LICENCE

If a marriage is to take place by licence, no publication of banns is necessary, provided that one of the parties has resided for not less than fifteen days in the parish where the church is situated. The ordinary Marriage Licence is granted by clerical officials known as Surrogates, or may be obtained by personal application to the diocesan Registry. The advantage of marriage by licence over marriage by banns is that the ceremony may take place as soon as the licence has been obtained. It is essential that one of the parties to be married should apply personally for a licence, as the applicant is required to sign a sworn declaration to the effect that there is no legal reason why the marriage should not take place, and that one of the parties of the marriage (if not both) has resided for at least fifteen days before the date of the application, within the parish of the church in which the marriage is to take place.

Licences (known as "Common Licences" as distinguished from "Special Licences") can be obtained from the Faculty Office, 1, The Sanctuary, Westminster, London, S.W.1, and used in any church which is licensed for weddings throughout England and Wales, provided the residence qualification has been kept. The Office of the Vicar-General, which is at the same address, grants licences for churches in the Province of Canterbury only; licences in the diocese of York are granted by the Vicar-General of the Province of York, Minster Yard, York. Licences are issued also at the Registries of the various Diocesan Bishops, which are situated in all cathedral cities. These licences can be used only in the diocese in which they are issued. The office of the Bishop of London is to be found at Dean's Court, Doctor's Commons, London, E.C.4.

SPECIAL LICENCES

A special licence permits a marriage to be solemnised on any date in any properly licensed church, but such licences are granted only by the Archbishop of Canterbury at the Faculty Office, 1, The Sanctuary, Westminster, London, S.W.1. The cost of a Special Licence is £25 (or more). Stamp Duty has been abolished. Before granting a special licence the Archbishop of Canterbury has to be satisfied that there is a sufficient reason why the ordinary marriage licence is unsuitable. When a special licence has been granted there is no restriction as to the residence of the parties or as to the time.

MARRIAGE BEFORE A REGISTRAR

If for any reason the couple decide to be married in a Registry Office, one of the parties to the marriage should call on the local Superintendent Registrar, or the Registrar of Marriages, who will make the necessary arrangements for the wedding to take place either by certificate or by licence.

In the first case an official form must be filled in, giving the names of the contracting parties, their ages and addresses, the address of the building at which the wedding is to take place, and concluding with a signed declaration that there is no legal objection to the marriage; and, in the case of those under age, that the consent of parents or of a magistrate has been obtained.

False information on this form would be severely punished. Both parties must have lived for seven days before the application within the area controlled by the Registrar; or if either lives in an area not under the control of the Registrar to whom the other party to the contract has applied, he or she must make a separate declaration before the Registrar controlling the district in which he or she has lived for seven days prior to the declaration. Having satisfied himself that the information given him is correct, the Superintendent Registrar will make the entry in the notice book and issue the certificate three weeks later.

The ceremony may then take place on any date within the three months following *the entry in the notice book, not within three months following the issue of the certificate.*

If the Registry Office wedding is to be by licence, the declaration to be made is similar, but only one of the contracting parties need apply to the Registrar, even if the other lives in a different registration area. It is, however, necessary for the one who makes the application to have lived in the area for fifteen days before applying for the licence.

The Superintendent Registrar, if satisfied with the information received, will make his entry in the notice book and issue the licence one clear day afterwards (not counting Sundays, Christmas Day and Good Friday). This licence holds good for three months.

It must be remembered that it is necessary to produce before the officiating Registrar, on the day of the ceremony, the certificate given by the Registrar (or by each Registrar if the parties live in different districts), or licence issued by the Registrar in whose area the application was accepted. The best man usually makes himself responsible for these papers.

Two people must be present at the wedding and sign their names as witnesses to the ceremony. They may be two strangers to the wedding couple or to each other.

NONCONFORMIST WEDDINGS

The requirements are similar to those mentioned above, and the duties are performed by the Registrar of Marriages, although nonconformist couples may be married in a chapel. By the Marriage Act of 1898, however, a Registrar is unnecessary when the chapel has been registered and has adopted the provisions of this Act, in which case the Minister or other authorised person may perform the duties usually reserved for the Registrar.

This applies throughout England and Wales. The ceremony is the same as that described in Chapter III.

ROMAN CATHOLIC WEDDINGS

A Roman Catholic wedding service is similar to that of the Protestant Church, except for the facts that the word "obey" is omitted and the bridegroom holds the right hand of his bride while saying "I ——— take thee ——— to be my wedded wife" and so on; but the ring is made more important in the ceremony, and the coins which the bridegroom presents to the bride symbolise the phrase "with all my worldly goods I thee endow". The bridegroom places the ring first upon the thumb of the bride's left hand, as he says "In the Name of the Father", transferring it to the index finger as he continues "and of the Son"; then to the next finger at the words "and of the Holy Ghost", finally placing it in position on the third finger as he says "Amen".

The ceremony concludes with prayers, including a very beautiful one for the bride's wisdom, love and peace.

JEWISH WEDDINGS

In Jewish weddings, couples are required to

give notice to the Registrar in the same way as is described under *Marriage before a Registrar*, but the marriage need not take place at the Registrar's Office; either a Synagogue or private house being used, according to the strictness of the couple's adherence to the Jewish Religious Laws. The only other legal point of variation is that a Jewish wedding may take place at any hour of the day, not necessarily before 6 p.m., as is required for other wedding ceremonies. A picturesque and symbolical part of the ceremony is the drinking of wine twice from the same vessel by each of the bridal couple, after which the husband drops the glass upon the ground and breaks it, to symbolise the irrevocability of the marriage.

QUAKER WEDDINGS

In Quaker weddings a ring is not strictly necessary at all, but the bridegroom usually presents his bride with a ring at the conclusion of the ceremony as a matter of expediency. The notice has to be given at a Friends' Meeting House, and a Registrar has to be in attendance to perform the legal essentials of the ceremony.

NAVAL WEDDINGS

Since the Naval Marriage Act of 1908, members

of the Royal Navy have been allowed special facilities owing to the difficulties which they naturally experience in fulfilling the residential requirements of the marriage notifications. Therefore it is permitted by the Act for any officer, seaman or marine aboard ship, to have the banns published by his commanding officer, or the ship's chaplain; or should the wedding be arranged to take place in a Registry Office or Nonconformist chapel the commanding officer may take the necessary particulars instead of the Registrar, issuing the required certificate after a lapse of twenty-one days.

Marriage by licence is not affected by this Act, but in either case the prospective bride must arrange matters on shore as already described.

ONE PARTY IN SCOTLAND

The person living in England or Wales acts exactly as already stated according to the form of marriage desired. The party living in Scotland must also give notice of marriage in accordance with the provisions described under the heading, *Scottish Marriages*.

Since the Marriage (Scotland) Act, 1939, notices issued in England and Wales are valid in Scotland, and *vice versa*, provided only one of the parties resides in Scotland. Note, however, that marriage by licence in a Registrar's Office in

England or Wales is not possible in these cases.

ONE PARTY IN IRELAND

The procedure is similar to that set out in the two preceding paragraphs except that, in Ireland, notice is given to the District Registrar of Marriages, while the residence qualification is seven days instead of fifteen days, as in Scotland.

SCOTTISH MARRIAGES

It should be noted that, by the laws of Scotland, a youth or a girl of and over the age of sixteen may contract a marriage without consent of parents or guardians.

Marriage in Scotland may only take place provided one or both of the parties have been resident there for fifteen days. It is important to remember that, under Scots law, the legal day is reckoned from midnight to midnight. In the case of a person who is not permanently domiciled in Scotland, the day of arrival and the day of departure do not count as part of the legal period of residence.

Since the Marriage (Scotland) Act, 1939, came into force on July 1st, 1940, irregular marriages by declaration in the presence of two witnesses and by other quaint methods are now invalid unless contracted before that date.

Marriages may be solemnized before a minister of one denomination or another in the presence of two witnesses aged sixteen years or over. It is required that one of the contracting parties must have been resident in Scotland for fifteen days immediately prior to giving notice of marriage, while the wedding must have been publicly proclaimed by banns or by "notice".

By law, the banns must be read in church on three consecutive Sundays; but common consent has long deemed one Sunday sufficient. The necessary certificate is then issued at a fee of 50p, and it is available for three months.

Marriage before a Registrar is now governed by the Marriage (Scotland) Act, 1939. When Notice of Marriage is given to a Registrar, he records particulars in his register on payment of a fee of £1, and the details of such entries are then posted up on the outer wall of his office. If both parties to the marriage live in the same parish or district, one notice, given jointly, is sufficient; but if the man and woman reside in different districts, each must give notice individually to their respective Registrars, and pay the fees for the entries of notice and certificates of due publication independently.

After the expiry of seven days, application must be made for a certificate of due publication which the Registrar will issue at a fee of 50p, provided nobody has lodged any objection which is likely to debar the marriage. Each party must obtain separate certificates if residing in different districts. The wedding may then take place at any time within three months.

On production of a Registrar's certificate or certificates of due publication in respect of both parties, the couple, in the presence of the Registrar and of two witnesses of the age of sixteen years or upwards, declare that they know of no legal impediment to their marriage and that they accept each other as husband and wife. The Registrar then issues a marriage certificate, in the form required by the Act, which is signed by the parties to the marriage, the Registrar and the two witnesses. The fee payable to the Registrar is £1.50. The marriage is valid unless there is a legal impediment.

The fee for a certificate of marriage contracted before either a Minister or a Registrar is 50p.

If a party is ill or some other unforeseen or exceptional circumstances prevent one of the parties from giving the required notice or arranging for the publication of banns within the time required, a joint application may be made to the Sheriff for a licence. If a Sheriff's licence is obtained, the marriage must take place within ten days of it being granted.

If a Quaker wedding is desired and either one or both parties is a member of or an attender associated with the Society of Friends, notice of marriage must be given to the local Registrar in the manner already described, and a certificate of due publication be obtained before the Quaker ceremony may take place.

Before a Jewish ceremony may be performed in Scotland, the same procedure as for Quakers applies, except that both parties must be members of the Jewish faith.

The Naval Marriages Act of 1908 applies to Scotland in exactly the same way as described previously for England and Wales.

Parties divorced under Scottish law may marry again immediately, as the Scottish decree is absolute from the time that a divorce is granted.

CHAPTER V

THE PARENTS' RESPONSIBILITIES

THE importance of the parents' duties towards
the bride is not to be regarded lightly. Most
fathers feel bound to make not only fullest
enquiries, if the suitor is comparatively a stranger,
or a new-comer in the neighbourhood, as to
character and financial standing, but will endeavour
to have a settlement large or small according
to their position, drawn up by his own solicitor,
and agreed to either by the bridegroom himself
or by his solicitors. This ensures, as far as possible,
the future financial safety of his daughter. Very
often, also, his wedding present takes the form
of a cheque. Usually, if the amount of the
settlement is a large one, the interest alone is
made payable to the bride in order that she
may be unable to draw on the capital either
for herself or her husband.

It is the duty of the bride's father to provide
the reception and the cars for guests proceeding
to and from the church, but not the car for the
use of the bridegroom.

The bride's father also is the proper person to

give the bride away, though in the case of a fatherless bride, her mother may do so, unless some male relative or friend is available; in that case the part of escorting the bride up the aisle should be also deputed to him. It is the bride's father (or his deputy) who drives with her to the church in the last car, and escorts her to her position at the chancel steps, after which he should retire a step or two to the left until the officiating clergyman pronounces the words "Who giveth this woman?" when he should advance and reply, "I do!"

When the bridal couple advance to the altar, he is at liberty to seat himself beside his wife (or bride's mother, as the case may be) in the front pew to the left of the aisle, until the wedded pair pass into the vestry to sign the register. Then it is his privilege to escort the bridegroom's mother to the vestry and down the aisle, leaving in the third car with her unless otherwise arranged beforehand; and if there should be a formal wedding breakfast, he sits on the bride's left with the bridegroom's mother next to him.

His formal dress should be similar to that of the bridegroom and best man.

When the wedding takes place in the country, accommodation should be provided for guests who are coming from some distance.

He usually makes the arrangements for this, friends and neighbours often volunteering to put up some of the wedding guests when his own house is filled to its utmost capacity; failing which, rooms must be taken at a local hotel.

The bride's mother, despite her very arduous and responsible duties in planning the wedding, takes very little part in the official ceremony, although her dress is very important, much noted and criticised, and generally reported on, next to that of the bride and bridesmaids. Her duties before the wedding consist of advising the bride throughout, assisting in ordering the trousseau, issuing the invitations, choosing guests, type of reception, refreshments, floral decorations, etc., and generally placing her experience, tact and good taste at the disposal of her daughter at this important epoch of her life.

She should leave the house together with such of the guests as are staying in the house. At the church she takes her place in the front pew to the left of the aisle, and at the conclusion of the ceremony she should walk with the bridegroom's father into the vestry and kiss the bride immediately after the newly-made husband, leaving with the groom's father, unless otherwise pre-arranged, by the car next to the bridal couple in order to greet the guests at the reception which follows. If there is a wedding breakfast, she will sit at the right of the bridegroom, with his father on her right.

THE DUTIES OF THE BRIDESMAIDS

Like those of the bride's mother, the duties of the chief bridesmaid are many and varied, although she takes a more official position than the former who, throughout, remains "the power behind the throne" and keeps well out of "the limelight".

It is the chief bridesmaid who is responsible for all the needs of the bride on the wedding morning, from gloves to orange-blossom. Prior to the wedding she has assisted the bride in the choice of clothes, including the dresses of the other bridesmaids for the ceremony, which are usually all alike, and chosen to harmonise in colour and type with the bride's wedding gown. If there are to be pages, the chief bridesmaid has also to see that their suits are of correct style.

She must also be willing to buy, choose, match colours, or order various small articles required for the wedding or even for the bride's new home.

On the wedding day, after assisting the bride to dress, if asked to do so, she will precede her to the church in order to be ready to arrange the group of bridesmaids and pages who follow the bride and her father as they advance to the altar.

Here she stands just behind the bride, a little to the left, holds her bouquet and gloves, when removed for the ring, arranges the bride's veil and train, and follows the parents and relatives on the arm of the best man as they all proceed to the vestry. After the register has been signed she also follows the married couple to the porch, and takes the fourth car, unless the order has been arranged otherwise beforehand.

During the reception she is placed near the bride, or manages to be frequently at her elbow in order to perform any little service required, and when it is time for the bride to change into her travelling costume, it is the chief bridesmaid who helps her to change—usually she is the only one of the bridesmaids to be in attendance at this little ceremony. Sometimes she performs the final service later of welcoming the honeymoon couple to their new home, after which her duties are, at last, at an end.

THE DUTIES OF THE BEST MAN

It is customary for a best man to be a bachelor, but this is not absolutely necessary, and any bridegroom who has a married chum is quite at liberty to choose him for his supporter. Indeed, the responsibilities of a best man are so important and numerous that it might be expected that a married man would make a better supporter than a bachelor, remembering his own experiences and needs.

As soon as the engaged couple have fixed the date of the wedding, and the style of ceremony required, he should discuss the arrangements, and from that moment until he sees the couple off on their honeymoon it will devolve upon him to ensure each necessary step being taken, and to ascertain that nothing has been forgotten. For this reason he must be prepared to give a good deal of time as well as thought and energy to the occasion. He will do well to enlist the services of several men friends as groomsmen. These will be of the utmost assistance to him, if they can be relied upon to usher guests to their places in church and escort them to their cars after the ceremony; assist the bridesmaids, and attend to the needs of the ladies at the reception.

Even the first interview with the officials of the church or Registry Office at which the wedding is to take place, may be greatly assisted and shortened by the presence of the best man, who is usually in a more business-like frame of mind than the bridegroom is likely to be.

It is essential for the best man to have extracted definite information from the engaged couple as to whether the service is to be choral, in which case hymns and wedding march must be chosen or discussed with the organist; whether the church is to be decorated with flowers, in which case it must be decided as to who will do it, and when it will be convenient for it to be done. He has to know also what fees are to be paid to the various church officials.

The best man will be wise, as well as kind, if he gives a little assistance to the bride's mother over the invitations, as these involve a good deal of discussion and clerical work.

The next point requiring his assistance will be the arrangements to be made for cars required on the wedding day. It is customary for the bride's father to provide and order those necessary to take the guests from the house to the church and then to the reception, but it is as well for the best man to ascertain that they actually have been booked. The bridegroom's car, as well as that used by the bridal pair on leaving for the honeymoon, should be ordered by the best man.

In the matter of dress, he must consult, assist and conform to the choice of the bridegroom. Formal wear for the best man comprises silk hat, black morning coat, grey waistcoat, striped trousers, black patent leather shoes, white shirt, stiff collar, grey tie and gloves, and white button-hole—usually a single flower, such as gardenia, carnation or rose. Should the wedding be at a Registry Office, or a quiet ceremony where the bride will wear her travelling costume, the bridegroom may wear a lounge suit or black coat and waistcoat with striped trousers and black bowler or grey felt hat, in which case the best man dresses similarly.

He will probably be wanted to accompany the bridegroom to the tailor, also to buy gloves, ties, collars, etc., required for the honeymoon as well as at the actual ceremony. He is often also requested to choose the bridegroom's wedding gifts to the bridesmaids. Above all, however, the best man should make certain that the bridegroom has the essential documents and the all-important wedding ring. The former will vary according to the particular type of ceremony to be performed, so that the best man would be well advised to study the previous chapter, which deals with the various marriage ceremonies, in order to obtain all necessary details for his friend's particular form of marriage. For example, if the couple are to be married by banns, and are living in different districts, it will be necessary to ensure that the banns are published in both districts, and to obtain a certificate from the clergyman of the church where the ceremony will *not* take place.

On the day of the wedding, the best man is expected to accompany the bridegroom on his way to the church, having first helped him to dress, and to take personal charge of any documents which may be wanted, as well as the wedding ring and a sufficient sum of money to cover fees, tips and other minor expenses.

The bridegroom and best man should reach the church at least a quarter of an hour before the time fixed for the wedding, and wait in the vestry until just before the bride is due to arrive, when they go into the church and seat themselves in the front pew on the right of the aisle until she appears. Then they should take their places for the ceremony, the best man at the right hand of the bridegroom and a little to the rear.

It is wise for him to take care of the bridegroom's hat and gloves, putting them with his own in some safe place where he can quickly reach them after the service.

When the service is concluded, the best man should give his left arm to the chief bridesmaid as they follow the bridal couple to the vestry to sign the register, where he usually acts as one of the witnesses to the signatures. He then hands the bridegroom his hat and gloves, and follows with the chief bridesmaid down the aisle to the porch, where he arranges the order in which the company are to drive to the reception.

Proceeding to the house or reception rooms, he still has the important part of Master of Ceremonies to fill by seeing the guests seated correctly, if it is a wedding breakfast, and handing refreshments to the ladies if they are served from a buffet. Also, it is he who must reply when the health of the bridesmaids is toasted.

When the bridegroom retires to change for the journey, he should see that the groom has all he needs, make sure that the car has arrived, and that the bridal couple's luggage is placed upon it, properly labelled if the journey is to be made by rail. If the latter has not been done, he must precede them to the station, have the labels affixed, and purchase the railway tickets. If guests are being entertained at the bride's residence, the best man is expected to return there after seeing off the honeymoon couple, otherwise his duties end when he waves them "goodbye".

Needless to say, the best man's expenses are repaid by the bridegroom when he returns from the honeymoon, unless a sufficient sum has been given to him beforehand to cover all out-goings, which is by far the more convenient plan.

Chapter VI

THE RECEPTION

AFTER the whole company has returned to the house, or arrived at the place appointed for the reception, the bride's mother takes up her position at the entrance of the reception room and greets the guests as they arrive, the bride and bridegroom being stationed in the centre of the room to receive the congratulations of the guests after they have greeted the bride's mother. Sometimes the presents are laid out for inspection, and as soon as the congratulations are over, refreshments should be served, usually at a buffet from which the best man and the male members of the party attend on the ladies, assisted by the servants or waiters. Savoury sandwiches (chicken, cucumber, egg and cress, etc.), cakes, tea, coffee, and wine comprise the usual menu, champagne being the traditional wine though by no means essential. If used, one bottle to every three persons is considered a good estimate.

In due course, the bride cuts the wedding cake. This is the appropriate moment for the champagne to be handed round, and everyone present must partake of the bridal cake.

It is a good plan, in order to avoid accidents, for the cake to have had the first piece partly cut but left in position for the bride to finish cutting. Absent friends should be sent a small piece with a wedding card in an ornamental box, but this is not done until a day or two after the ceremony —another little duty for the bride's mother.

If a luncheon or an elaborate wedding breakfast is provided, the bride and bridegroom seat themselves at the head of the table, the bridegroom on the right of his bride. At his right hand sits the bride's mother, with his father next to her; and on the bride's left sits her father, with her husband's mother next to him. Although described as a "breakfast" the conventional wedding feast usually consists of soup, fish, entrées, joints and poultry, sweets, cheese, dessert and coffee.

Should the reception take the form of an afternoon tea, speeches should be short and informal, and toasts are not generally drunk.

The bridegroom should reply to the chief toast or speech including, in his response, his appreciation of the assistance given by the bridesmaids, unless a separate toast or speech is given in honour of the latter; then, the best man replies for them. All speeches should be brief, as the bride has many congratulatory friends and relatives to speak to before she is gently extricated by the chief bridesmaid in order to change into her travelling costume. The chief bridesmaid is the only one to assist her in this ceremony, and it is then that the bride can seize the opportunity to bid her parents "good-bye" in private. At the same time, or a little later, the bridegroom retires to change into a lounge suit for the journey.

The time fixed for "retiring to change" should be a little over an hour after the time appointed for the reception, so as to give a little margin for farewells before starting on the honeymoon.

All the guests should remain until the bride and bridegroom have departed on their honeymoon. The old-fashioned customs of throwing confetti, rice and even an old slipper after the bridal pair, are gradually falling into disfavour, though just a few people may scatter the newer silver-paper horseshoes for "luck".

A short account of the event should be sent by the bride's parents to the editor of the local newspaper, unless it has been ascertained that a reporter was present.

TOASTS AND SPEECHES AT THE RECEPTION

Though perhaps the most difficult and unappreciated efforts of all the details of a wedding, toasts and speeches are definitely a necessary part of the formal proceedings, and can best be made helpful by being brief, appropriate and to the point.

TO THE BRIDEGROOM

It is hardly necessary to remind the bride's father, whose duty it is to rise and propose the health of the bride and bridegroom, that the newly-married couple are probably feeling quite sufficiently embarrassed and nervous without more public allusions to their position than are absolutely necessary. He will therefore be wise and kind to reduce his speech to the utmost limits of brevity consistent with politeness, and a one or two-minute speech will readily meet the occasion.

The speech quoted below may serve as an example of the "one-minute" type.

"Ladies and Gentlemen,

May I claim your attention for a moment while I perform the most pleasurable duty and privilege on this happy occasion, which is to speed on their way the fortunate pair who have today set sail upon the Sea of Matrimony. May their life's skies always look as serenely blue and smiling as they do today; may storms be brief, and their ship of love come safely to harbour in the Islands of the Blest.

"Ladies and Gentlemen, let us drink to the long life, prosperity and happiness of the bride and bridegroom."

THE BRIDEGROOM'S REPLY

The bridegroom is not expected to be in a state

of mind to deliver an oration, but may take the opportunity of mentioning the consideration with which the bride's family have treated him.

The following reply is one of the "short and sweet" type which was much appreciated by listeners for that reason.

"Ladies and Gentlemen,

I thank you for the kindness and help which you have given me in making this day so memorable and happy. I should like to take this opportunity of thanking my dear wife's parents (who are now mine also) for their unfailing consideration during the time of our courtship and engagement. On behalf of my wife and myself I thank the ladies who have lent their presence and assistance to grace the occasion, and the best man for his loyal support.

"I wish also to heartily congratulate one person present in having won 'the fairest flower of all', and that is—myself.

"Ladies and Gentlemen, thank you, one and all, very much indeed."

The bride is seldom expected to make a speech but may do so if she wishes to add her thanks to those of her husband, or remain silent and smile her acknowledgments. It is perhaps more gracious if she just says, "I think you have all been very kind, and I thank you very much".

THE HEALTH OF THE BRIDESMAIDS

This toast is proposed by the bridegroom in many cases; but should he not do so, the bridesmaids should be toasted by some prominent gentlemen of the company *other* than the best man, who has to reply for them.

A few brief words in congratulation, such as follows, comprise all that is really necessary.

"Ladies and Gentlemen,

It is my very pleasant duty to propose the health of the bridesmaids. I am requested by the bride to express her gratitude to all, especially to the chief bridesmaid, Miss ———.

"As for the ornamental value given to the ceremony by these young ladies, well, I need only add, 'Look at them and tremble for the continued bachelorhood of the best man'. "

THE BEST MAN REPLIES

"Ladies and Gentlemen,

On behalf of the bridesmaids, I thank you all very much for your kind appreciation, with which I heartily agree. The duties of best man are, I assure you, extremely hard with all these distracting creatures to keep his eye on as well as the bridegroom; however, this experience may stand me in good stead as a kind of understudy for the principal part which I am evidently fated to take at some future time.

"Ladies and Gentlemen, thank you very much."

Chapter VII

THE HONEYMOON ARRANGEMENTS

THE planning of the honeymoon trip is perhaps the most pleasant task of all the wedding arrangements, and should be decided upon and estimated well in advance of the ceremony, as last-minute bookings and haphazard holidays are likely to prove unsatisfactory, owing to the most comfortable berths, rooms or other accommodation, being already booked up for the dates required.

The choice of a honeymoon resort naturally depends on the tastes and means of each bridal couple. However, all newly married couples have one desire in common: to be, as far as possible, on their own. For a complete breakaway from everyday surroundings many couples spend their honeymoons abroad; and the Continent has the added attraction that it provides good holidays at every season of the year.

Paris in the spring is a traditional honeymoon choice, and a fortnight may well be divided between the French capital and one of the watering places on the northern coast, such as Dinard, Dieppe, or Trouville.

Another ideal spring honeymoon is a tour among the flower fields of Holland, blazing with tulips and hyacinths. This is especially suitable for a couple interested in picturesque architecture, quaintly dressed people and curious customs.

For those whose honeymoon falls in wintertime there is an obvious attraction in the winter-sports centres in Switzerland. The best time for this sort of holiday is between Christmas and the end of February. There are similar winter-sports centres in the French Alps.

For those who prefer a more restful honeymoon there are ideal winter resorts on the sunny French Riviera. Although it is fashionable, a holiday on the Riviera need not be unduly expensive provided the couple are content to stay in one of the numerous hotels of modest price. The best centre for excursions is Nice, which is only a few miles from Monte Carlo and the Italian frontier.

In the summer the Continent offers a very wide range of attractions, with resorts to suit every taste. For those who like a sea-voyage Scandinavia has an obvious appeal; while those who can afford to travel by air can spend a delightful fortnight in far-off places such as southern Italy. All honeymoons abroad can be arranged through travel agencies.

For those who do not want to go abroad there are all kinds of ways of spending a honeymoom in Britain without going near a seaside boarding-house. In spring a motoring or cycling tour through Cornwall, Devon and the southern counties will provide a feast of beauty; while in summer the motorists, cyclists, and hikers have a fine choice of territory. The Lake District offers scenery unsurpassed anywhere on the Continent; Wales and Scotland have attractions for mountain-climbers; and those who want a honeymoon afloat need look no farther than the Norfolk Broads.

It is wise to map out the direction and nature of the honeymoon trip before completing the bride's trousseau; for instance, a walking tour on the Yorkshire Moors would entail the inclusion of low-heeled shoes and a tweed coat and skirt in the list of garments, while a cruise in sunny waters would provide the necessity for deck sports suits and summer dresses.

The bridegroom, too, will need to order his outfit as soon as the honeymoon trip has been decided upon, as happiness depends so much more upon comfort and suitability of clothes than an engaged young man is likely to realise. He should endeavour, therefore, to plan all accommodation necessary from start to finish, well in advance, whether it is in hotel, boarding-house, boat or plane, as only by thinking out every detail before-hand can worry and discomfort be avoided.

Most couples expect to find their own company and the various amusements offered by the journey sufficient to keep them interested from start to finish, but it is a wise pair who decide to pack one or two diversions for odd half-hours or a rainy afternoon, such as a few novels by a favourite author, golf clubs, skis or rackets, and the necessary sporting kit if either or both are devoted to any of these sports.

A honeymoon is such a tremendous additional expense at a time when a large amount of expenditure has been already unavoidable, that many young couples decide to dispense with it altogether in order to start the new home with a good reserve fund for emergencies. This is, of course, a purely personal matter which should concern none but themselves; but should they agree to shorten or forgo the honeymoon, the young wife's social duties commence practically at once, and it is customary for one to ignore the fact that the young couple are only just married and call, leaving cards, and send invitations and so on almost immediately.

THE NEW HOME

The problem of setting up the new home resolves itself into the question either of renting a house in a neighbourhood which seems suitable, or buying a house in which to settle permanently.

Should the husband's means of livelihood be one which may require him to remove his abode from one district to another from time to time, then rental of suitable accommodation is advisable to save much trouble and expense; and though in many parts of the country, houses and flats to be let are few and far between, when available they can usually be rented on short term agreements of one, three, or more years, rendering removal comparatively easy. When, however, a permanent home is desired, then the house can usually be bought through the help of a Building Society, which, although adding considerably to the cost, works out cheaper than rent, and does not necessitate disturbing capital.

This is, however, a matter for personal decision between the young couple. Should the decision be on the side of buying a house through a Building Society, there is much to recommend the method as long as a reliable society of good standing is chosen, and the borrower is reasonably certain of being able to repay the loan in regular instalments, for it has the advantage of providing an asset at the end of the agreed term of years.

A loan is granted by most societies for a fixed term of years up to twenty-five, with the amount repayable by equal monthly instalments consisting partly of capital, partly of interest on the balance of mortgage debt outstanding. The total amount payable over the period covers the original advance, together with the total interest charged year by year. The interest included in the payments and charged each year is now about

8 per cent., but this rate is variable in relation to the Bank Rate. Borrowers are entitled to relief of income tax on the amount paid in interest each year.

Most societies will usually grant advances to prospective purchasers of suitable freehold property, up to 80 per cent. of the purchase price, or the society's estimate of value for mortgage purposes, whichever is the lower. Where the security offered is exceptionally acceptable, even a larger proportion may be advanced. In the case of a purchase for private occupation, an approved Indemnity Policy issued by an Insurance Company will be acceptable by most societies to cover excess advances up to a maximum of 90 per cent. of the valuation of the house.

Acceptable forms of security may be:

1. Title deeds of other property.
2. Life Policy possessing an adequate surrender value.
3. Agreed Cash Deposit.
4. Government or Municipal Corporation Stocks.
5. Important Stock Exchange Securities.

As an example, if it is proposed to buy a house and spread the mortgage over 25 years, the scale of payment per £100 is 78p per calendar month, and is so calculated as to make the sum repaid lessen in interest but increasing in the amount of the loan paid off, till the final payment is the last amount of loan.

There are other methods of obtaining an advance on house property. Sometimes a private loan can be obtained on such terms are these: a loan of £800 is made, repayable in eight years at the rate of 8 per cent. per annum. By the end of the first year, £100 of the loan and £64 in interest should have been paid, but at the end of the second year it should be necessary only to pay £100 of the loan and £56 interest as the capital sum has now been reduced to £700, and so on, the interest being reduced by £8 each year as there is £100 less loan to pay for. It may be arranged also that the repayments are made in equal instalments at more frequent intervals than yearly or half-yearly.

There is also the method of purchasing a house on the instalment plan by applying to the local authorities for assistance under the terms of the Housing Act of 1949. Under this Act local authorities are empowered to grant loans to persons buying houses for their own occupation provided the market value does not exceed a certain fixed amount.

Each local authority can set up, within certain limits, its own code of rules governing the loan, therefore application has to be made to the authority in the desired district to obtain the terms and rate of interest. The advantage to be gained lies in the fact that this rate is considerably lower than under any other purchasing plan, as there is no desire to make commercial gain from the transaction. The term may also be extended to thirty years.

There are yet other ways of arranging a mortgage for house purchase, but space does not permit their inclusion here. They are, however, fully discussed in *Wedding Etiquette* by Mary Woodman, published by W. Foulsham & Co., Ltd.

Chapter VIII

WEDDING SYMBOLS

Of all the insignia of love and marriage, there is no symbol more important or interwoven with sentiment than the golden circlet with which the union is sealed, yet by an Act of Parliament passed in 1837, a marriage legally may take place without it. Tradition and sentiment alone have made it more essential to the bride than her wedding gown, veil or even the altar. Its circular shape, without beginning or end, is an emblem of perfect union, the merging of two entities; its substance, gold, being chosen not only because it is the most precious metal, but because like true love, wear only brightens and polishes its shining surface.

Herrick describes it:

"And as this round is nowhere found to flaw, or else to sever; so let our love as endless prove, and pure as gold for ever".

It is placed on the third finger of the bride's left hand, tradition has it, because a vein connected with the heart reaches to the root of that finger. In reality that is neither correct, nor the true origin of the custom, which was that the third finger, being less in actual use than any of the others, is protected on each side and more or less hidden from danger.

The veil dates back to ancient times when both the bride and bridegroom were screened from the gaze of the curious by a thin canopy of gauze. The bridegrooms of today are possibly bolder, or else too happy to be conscious of public scrutiny.

The bridal bouquet also signifies more than a mere personal adornment, for in olden times it formed part of a wreath which was worn on any momentous occasion, marriage being considered only one of them.

The orange-blossom, symbol of innocence, was grown originally in the Holy Land, where it signified purity and religious piety.

The confetti or rice thrown from the church door symbolised a full harvest which was the wish of the newly-married couple's friends.

The old shoe thrown after or tied to the departing car, is a custom which is dying out now. Curiously enough it originated in the Anglo-Saxon custom whereby the father of the bride had to give one of her shoes to the newly-made husband, who touched his wife lightly on the head with the tip of it to signify that he was to be, in future, her lord and master.

It is interesting to note that in the East the

marriage service is known as the "Crowning".

Lastly, the wedding cake. This is really the symbol of wedded prosperity which dates back to Roman times when the bride ate a piece of cake made from flour and water to signify the hope that they would never lack the vital necessities of life. From this simple fare has evolved the elaborate wedding cake of modern times.

WEDDING SUPERSTITIONS

There is a fashion in superstitions just as there is in the style of the wedding dress, and the trend of the moment is extremist; either the folk-lore of marriage is to be flouted entirely, as when a modern bride chooses to be married in a green wedding dress, or followed with a slavishness almost absurd in this age of enlightenment.

Whichever the young bride chooses to do, however, there is no doubt as to the interest aroused by the traditions of luck or the reverse attached to various colours, mascots and omens.

Perhaps the oldest wedding rhyme known is the one which advises the bride to wear:

Something old and something new,
Something borrowed and something blue,

for luck on her wedding day.

Another old rhyme is attached to the days of the week:

> Monday for health,
> Tuesday for wealth,
> Wednesday's the best of all.
> Thursday brings crosses,
> And Friday losses,
> But Saturday—no luck at all.

As regards the month, it is supposed to be unlucky to marry in May or wear a green wedding dress.

> Marry in May, unhappy for Aye.

It is considered unlucky to marry on a Friday, especially if it is the 13th of the month.

As to the colour of the wedding gown:

> Married in white,
> You have chosen aright.
> Married in blue,
> Your lover is true.
> Married in pink,
> Your fortunes will sink.
> Married in green,
> You will not long be seen.
> Married in red,
> You'll wish you were dead.
> Married in yellow,
> Ashamed of the fellow.
> Married in brown,
> You'll live out of town.

Married in grey,
You'll live far away.
Married in black,
You'll wish you were back.

A widow should not marry in white, nor a maiden in colours.

It is unlucky to wear either pearls or opals with the bridal dress, also to postpone the wedding day.

There is a better reason for choosing white than the one given in the old rhyme, and that is the fact that it symbolises purity. Green typifies youth; red, courage; violet, modesty; blue, spiritual affinity. Yellow is the colour symbolical of jealousy, and few brides would choose it. One fancies that the lines of the jingle are more chosen for their rhyming quality than the actual truth of the superstition.

In regard to the months, February, June, the "month of roses", August, September, November and December are considered the lucky months in which to marry, and the bridegroom's birthday the luckiest of dates for the wedding.

As to weather, the omens are very contradictory, but the best known saying is:

"Happy is the bride whom the sun shines on".

However, German brides believe that every drop of rain which falls on the wedding day brings a blessing with it.

It is fortunate for a bride to meet a lamb, a dove, a spider, or a black cat on her way to church; but a pig or a funeral are bad omens, and country brides fear the crowing of a cock after dawn of the wedding day.

One of the few superstitions affecting the bride-groom is that he should not see his bride on the wedding day until he meets her at the altar.

A superstition about names runs:
Change the name and not the letter,
You'll change for worse and not for better.

Other well-known bridal customs include the "telling of the bees" and on country farms where bees are kept, they are not only told of the marriage but given some of the wedding cake as well.

It is supposed to be unlucky for the bride to try on the wedding dress or the veil for the bridegroom to see before the wedding day. A bride should throw away every pin when removing her dress and veil, or she will be unlucky. If she wishes to be the dominating influence in her married life, she must be the first of the two to buy something after the marriage. The best way to ensure this is to buy a pin from her chief bridesmaid when changing into her travelling costume.

After the wedding, the bride should break up her bouquet, tossing the flowers amongst the bridesmaids and girl friends. Whoever catches one of the blooms may expect to be married before another year has passed.

The best man should ensure good luck to the couple by giving an odd sum of money to the clergyman for his fee, and seeing that the bridegroom carries a small mascot in his pocket. He must not allow the latter to turn back for anything after the wedding journey has been started.

After the honeymoon, the husband should carry his wife over the threshold of their new home in order to bring good fortune on their future life.

WEDDING ANNIVERSARIES

Except for the well-known silver and golden weddings, very little notice is taken of wedding anniversaries except perhaps between the married couple themselves; but as these constitute the very people who will naturally be most interested, a list is appended of the various articles or materials associated by tradition with each anniversary. Even these vary a little in different parts of the country, but this difficulty can be surmounted by giving a gift of both articles, or letting the bride take her choice of the gift in which the appropriate article figures.

1st Anniversary	Cotton Wedding.
2nd „	Paper Wedding.
3rd „	Leather or Straw Wedding.

5th Anniversary	Wooden Wedding.
7th ,,	Woollen Wedding.
10th ,,	Tin Wedding.
12th ,,	Linen or Silk Wedding.
15th ,,	Crystal Wedding.
20th ,,	China Wedding.
25th ,,	SILVER WEDDING.
30th ,,	Pearl or Ivory Wedding.
40th ,,	Ruby Wedding.
50th ,,	GOLDEN WEDDING.
60th & 75th ,,	DIAMOND WEDDING.

Chapter IX

LEGAL FORMALITIES

CERTAIN legal matters of importance to the newly married couple's joint interests should be known and acted upon by the husband, primarily the question of his will, which unless legally in order may cause unsuspected difficulties should anything unforeseen occur.

At one time (before the Law of Property Act of 1925) a will made before marriage was revoked after the ceremony, but now if a will shows clearly that it is drawn up by a person in view of his or her approaching marriage, it is legally in order.

The form of will made by one in contemplation of marriage should be somewhat as follows:

This is the last Will and Testament of me Andrew Bell of Beverley Court Kensington in the County of Middlesex Merchant made in contemplation of my marriage with Alice Moore of 80 Queen's Terrace Bayswater spinster I appoint the said Alice Moore sole executrix of this my will and I devise and bequeath all my property unto her absolutely

In witness thereof I have hereunto set my
hand this first day of March One Thousand
Nine Hundred and —— ——

(Signed) ANDREW BELL

Signed by the above as his last will in the
presence of us both at the same time who at his
request and in his presence and in the presence
of each other have hereunto subscribed our
names as witnesses

ALFRED JONES (Clerk)
10 Lord's Lane, Sutton, Surrey.

GEORGE BARKER (Clerk)
27 The Avenue, Richmond, Surrey.

The entire absence of punctuation should be
noted and the simple form of wording retained
as involved sentences are liable to have a legal
interpretation which may not be exactly what was
intended.

Should the husband, in the press of his other
preparations for the wedding, neglect making his
will until the day of the wedding itself, it is
advisable to word it so that it is quite clear that
the will was drawn up after the ceremony which
joined the husband and wife in matrimony.

The following addition after the usual attestation clause to be signed by the witnesses will ensure this:

And which signature by the said Andrew Bell and subscription by us took place between the hours of two and three o'clock in the afternoon of Thursday the eighteenth of June One Thousand Nine Hundred and —————— immediately after the solemnisation on that day of the ceremony of marriage between the said Andrew Bell and Alice Moore now his wife.

Should the important document have been left until after the honeymoon, it should be seen to without further delay and the following wording used:

This is the last Will and Testament of me Andrew Bell of Beverley Court Kensington in the County of Middlesex Merchant I devise and bequeath all my property unto my wife Alice absolutely and I appoint her to be the sole executrix of this my will In witness whereof I have hereunto set my hand this sixteenth day of April One Thousand Nine Hundred and ——————

(Signed) ANDREW BELL

Signed by the above Andrew Bell as his last will in the presence of us both at the same time who at his request and in his presence and in the presence of each other have hereunto subscribed our names as witnesses

ALFRED JONES (Clerk)
10 Lord's Lane, Sutton, Surrey.

GEORGE BARKER (Clerk)
27 The Avenue, Richmond, Surrey.

INSURANCES

Another important matter for the husband to consider is the question of taking out a life insurance. His new responsibilities make it necessary, as if he should die without having made due provision for her, his wife would suffer financially, and it is to safeguard her in the event of his death that the life policy is designed. It is a great mistake to delay the matter, as the longer he leaves it the larger will be the amount of the annual premiums he will have to pay in order to secure reasonable benefits; meanwhile, should he die, his widow would be left unprovided for. Trustworthy people can generally be found to advise him as to the best insurance company to choose.

It is important to ascertain that the policy taken out is fully guaranteed from the moment that the first premium is paid. The amount for which the policy is taken out depends, of course, upon the financial position of the married couple, but any amount below £500 is of little use, and a rebate of Income Tax being granted on the premium paid is an assistance in the case of a husband whose income is small.

Policies against danger of fire, burglary and loss should also be taken out, and most companies issue what is termed an "All-in" policy in which all contingencies are covered, the premiums being very low.

Many people like to take out Endowment Policies also, by which sums are paid on reaching a certain age. There is also the question of annuities to be studied. All these points should be gone into as soon as possible after the return from the honeymoon.

RELATIONS WHO MAY NOT MARRY

Under the heading of "A table of kindred and affinity wherein whosoever are related are forbidden in Scripture and our laws to marry together", the Prayer Book gives the following list:

1. A man may not marry his grandmother, grandfather's wife, wife's grandmother, father's sister, mother's sister, father's brother's wife, mother's brother's wife, wife's father's sister, wife's mother's sister, mother, stepmother, wife's mother, daughter, wife's daughter, son's wife, sister, wife's sister, if the wife had been divorced and was still living, brother's wife, son's daughter, daughter's daughter, son's son's wife, daughter's son's wife,

wife's son's daughter, wife's daughter's daughter, brother's daughter, sister's daughter, brother's son's wife, sister's son's wife, wife's brother's daughter, and wife's sister's daughter.

2. A woman may not marry with her grandfather, grandmother's husband, husband's grandfather, father's brother, mother's brother, father's sister's husband, mother's sister's husband, husband's father's brother, husband's mother's brother, father, stepfather, husband's father, son, husband's son, son's daughter's husband, daughter's daughter's husband, husband's son's son, husband's daughter's son, brother's son, sister's son, brother's daughter's husband, sister's daughter's husband, husband's brother's son and husband's sister's son.

Most of the above relationships are so obviously barred as to be without interest, but occasionally cases arise in which people wishing to marry do come within one of the affinities set out in the Prayer Book. Usually it is a husband who desires to marry his wife's sister, or a wife, her husband's brother.

An Act of Parliament in 1907 made it legal for a man to marry his *deceased* wife's sister, or *deceased* brother's wife; while an Act of 1921 gave similar consent to a woman marrying her *deceased* husband's brother, or her *deceased* sister's husband. At the same time, Parliament recognised that it might offend the conscience of a clergyman to solemnise marriage between two people of these relationships, so he was accorded the right to refuse; but that right was not given to the Superintendent of Registrars, to whom all couples, falling under the possible disapproval of the Church, should apply.

FOULSHAM'S
POCKET   LIBRARY